Business & Pleasure

Have Your Cake and Eat It Too.

The Entrepreneurs Daily Motto:

"We are forged from Our no's, driven from our naysayers, inspired when there's no inspiration, embraced when there's no help, leaned upon when there's no more shoulders. Yes, we weep but not for long, yes, we stumble but not for long, yes, I am down but not for long. We stand up to the challenge because we are entrepreneurs, and we will rise to the occasion."

Copyright © 2022 by Mr. Gentleman

All rights reserved. No part of this book may be reproduced or used in any manner without written permission of the copyright owner except for the use of quotations in a book review.

This book is dedicated to the grass root entrepreneurs who continually grind through the struggles of everyday life.

Contents

INTRODUCTION 7

CHAPTER ONE 1

Partnership 1

    Partnership in marriage 2

    Partnership in business 6

CHAPTER TWO 9

SHOULD YOU GO INTO BUSINESS WITH YOUR MARRIAGE PARTNER? 9

    Benefits of working with your marriage partner 10

    The challenges of working together with your marriage partner 13

    Phases of partnering with your marriage partner 15

CHAPTER THREE 17

LEADERSHIP AND FAMILY; SELF-REFLECTION 17

CHAPTER FOUR 22

TIME MANAGEMENT 22

    Time management strategies for couples working together 24

    Advantages of time management for couples working together 27

Most important principles of time management.................31

CHAPTER FIVE..35

THE SMART MOVE 35

    Setting boundaries 35

CHAPTER SIX 42

STORIES FROM SUCCESSFUL BUSINESSES MANAGED BY COUPLES (CASE STUDY; Cathy and Jeffrey, Vernic and Mitesh, David and Nicole) 42

    ☐ Cathy and Jeffrey, The owners of Hillrock Estate Distillery..42

    Vernic & Mitesh, Founders of PlantOGram......................44

    David and Nicole, The Cookie Cups................................46

CHAPTER SEVEN...48

THE BUSINESS AND PLEASURE BALANCE RESPONSIBILITIES...48

    Show more extraordinary passion and enthusiasm toward your relationship...48

    Signs of a passionate couple working together 51

    Be eager to apologize. 53

        Essential to apologize sincerely to your partner 54

    Learn to forgive 56

Be open to communication. 58
Why is communication important in relationships? 58
Communication skills for relationships 60
Role clarity 63
Love and Finances 68
CONCLUSION 73

INTRODUCTION

"Remember to enjoy your life, your family, and those you call friends. You owe it to not just yourself but humanity. Experience every day like it has to be lived or your time will not count"- Michael Carpenter.

A fulfilled life is often based on how well you contribute and live with others, especially managing your home. A life of tenacity and pleasure is the best balance you can attain to live a purposeful life. But how true is it? Do you find stability with work and your love when you work with your partner?

"Your process may be messy, but your mess will become your message"

The good thing is to complement each other well. Making your partners strength to be your weakness and vice versa. It's not abnormal to see things from a completely different perspective with your partner and challenge each other's idea, the amazing thing is to fall somewhere in the middle at the end of the day.

If you are thinking about working with your spouse or are in it already, you need to realize that staying as a business partner with your marriage partner requires you to understand a lot of things

A look at some relationship factors emphasized on to make you manage your business and pleasure is compatibility and love. These two factors play a major role in being the best in every aspect of your life. They allow you to see yourself and your partner as an entity. You get to do things together and enjoy it without being bored. Working together makes the journey easier and faster. The quote that says *two heads are better than one* has a good reason to tell you that.

Compatibility with good intention can go as far as to sustain your relationship beyond love. Love is what brings you together but isn't what keeps you together. Therefore, people divorce or break up when they start working with someone they love. But with compatibility, the rate at which you endure each other's flaws will be easier. Compatibility brings about understanding; the more you understand each other, the better the love grows.

There are ups and downs to owning a business with your spouse. It's one thing to own a business with your spouse, and it is another to be satisfied with long-term success at home and in the office. Long-term success is the best result of your partnership's total dedication, both at work and outside of it. 60% of husband-and-wife enterprises fail because they didn't get to know what's normal and what's abnormal in this scenario.

In this book, you'll find motivational quotes written by me that can help you in your journey. Let's dive right in!

"The greatest hazard in life is to risk nothing."

CHAPTER ONE

Partnership

"A man may do an immense deal of good, if he does not care who gets the credit for it."

Before I dig into the moves and the understanding you need to start or continue a business with your spouse, I'll like to explain partnership here. The term partnership is a legal mode of operation and arrangement between two or more people to achieve a common goal and share the risks and benefits. Partnership involves agreement and requires the utmost commitment to do business; in this context, marriage grows and yields valuable results. The term partnership is way heftier than how we characterize it. A partnership is weightier than a relationship because of *"commitment."*

Partnership inputs commitment to a relationship and allows you to see what is necessary to grow, which is why it's essential for any relationship development. Partnerships allow the partners to take responsibility since something important is at stake. You don't want to lose that value and the aim you both want to achieve. Based on the context of this course, we will briefly discuss two types of partnership which includes the

- Partnership in marriage
- Partnership in business

Partnership in marriage

Since you understand that partners have equal power and responsibility to shoulder for their goals to be achieved, so is it also in a marriage relationship setting. Both partners have equal power over the decisions in the relationship. It's not an authoritarian system but one where you both make unified decisions to promote the relationship's growth. This method allows respect and confidence in each other to believe that you are doing what you can to help the team. Both partners feel respected and that their voice is heard in the relationship.

Mr. Gentleman

Marriage should be treated as a partnership where you can decide on the family's growth and preparedness for what the future holds.

There's a mentality that should be included in any family, especially for the upcoming kids, on how to treat their spouse. This can be shown by the parents so that the kids can learn how to treat their partners in years to come. When it comes to house chores, they should be allocated according to their capability level; the same goes for financial aspects and other important factors needed in a relationship. Once it becomes one-sided, one of the partners will surely feel suppressed, unappreciated, and unhappy. Both partners need equal distribution and quotas they should follow. This doesn't mean that each chore and activity should be split equally but according to one another's capability.

I have encountered many partners in marriage relationships, and a major complaint I learned is that they are not well appreciated for what they bring to their relationships, especially the female gender because they carry more responsibility. Upon taking a critical and deep look into the disorder, I noticed that these behaviors seen in any relationship have existed for quite a long time and can even be traced as far back as the fellows' upbringing. The way we are raised has a significant effect on how we treat our partners.

A family where the orders and decisions solely rest on the father, or the mother can also be visible when you choose to make all the decisions as a husband or Father. A Family where you, as a daughter, grew up in a family where the female or the man's voice is unheard, which can also be seen in how reluctant you are to voice your point of view.

For equality and self-respect to be practiced in a relationship, certain values, beliefs, and goals must be followed so you both can know when you fault it. There are certain things that you must fit in for your marriage relationship to work out. Don't allow love only to sustain your relationship; it takes a bigger sacrifice and commitment to stick to it. I will further explain more about these sets of characteristics as we go through this course.

"I just hope I provide the love that my children need to nature healthy growth. I want my children to see I provide their mother with that body, mind and soul felt love. I want

my children to watch mom and dad dance in the kitchen after dinner and see shivery isn't dead and feel love is in the air. I want productive human beings who knows right from wrong, hard work is required, and they can be anything in life regardless of race, gender, or background. Listen more than they speak, judge everyone accordingly regardless of lifestyle choices, or society designated social class. I just hope I instill the love that not only makes them feel whole but eternal true love. I want my children to understand that I will always be there king but understand that they need their future Prince. And most of all show that it's beyond acceptable even today in life to... Love to Love."

Business and Pleasure; eat your cake and have it

Partnership in business

According to a US study by the National Academy of Sciences, 22% of US couples met at their workplace. There's been an increase in the rate at which co-workers get into a romantic relationship and eventually tie the knot. But it's always unpleasant after a few years since they rarely see each other often.

One of the unpleasant circumstances often encountered is the risk of putting your business as a priority rather than the family or relationship. Most times, the discussion is solely based on the workplace, deadlines they both must hit, and their focus is always on work which affects their romantic life. Such a disorder requires a rethink about how to plan things. They could plan a date to strengthen their relationship and lay off work matters at home.

"I will take action when others hesitate, I will outwork my competition"

As partners also at the workplace with your spouse, many disputes might have occurred right at home or work and affect how you respond, which is a big challenge many people feel. Some boundaries deserve each other's respect and should be maintained in order not to bring house problems to the workplace; there are ways you call each other to show professionalism, there are things you can only discuss at the workplace, and many other things that should be made distinct clear if you are to enjoy your work and relationship at the same time.

> *"It's okay to be unbalanced for a while. To be the best in the world at what you do you have to be unbalanced to find every bit of energy and strength to pull it off. Then you become balanced when you pull it off"*

As an entrepreneur, you should know that entrepreneurship demands a careful balance between your business and personal life. But a whole other set of difficulties can arise when you co-own a prosperous company with your spouse. Your marriage and your business will be impacted by the problems you will face. And a prosperous company without a prosperous home is only enjoying the length of time as it will soon be affected by what the couples are facing at home. This brings about the question a lot of entrepreneurs are finding the correct answer to; is it safe to launch a business with my marriage partner?

CHAPTER TWO

SHOULD YOU GO INTO BUSINESS WITH YOUR MARRIAGE PARTNER?

"When you face obstacles when you face bumps in the road, when you feel like you can't go on anymore take that as a challenge and compete against not anyone but yourself it's a beautiful thing when you take your obstacles and turn it into a challenge that you will overcome and succeed."

Have you discussed forming a business partnership with your spouse and need to figure out how well it will go? Or you discovered a potential in your marriage, and you think it will be necessary for both of you to be professional partners?

Starting a business with your spouse can be tough and extremely rewarding. You'll have an old buddy as your business partner, which can help you build on each other's advantages and divide the labor.

"To survive the unsurvivable there is always a way"

While working together in a partnership with your spouse to run a firm has its advantages, there are also disadvantages. In short, this can be a blessing when used correctly, but it can also be something else when misused. However, this must be appropriately approached if you want to connect and advance personally and professionally, i.e., in business and pleasure. This book will help you through the hurdles and benefits of running a business with your marriage partner.

"There is always a way, when things look like no way there is a way to do the impossible "

Benefits of working with your marriage partner

"What if you stop listening to the wrong people, and start listening to the right people and let their voice be louder "

Let's go over the benefits you can derive from running a business with your marriage partner:

- **Honest dialogue**

Effective communication is essential to any successful collaboration, whether it's a romantic relationship or a business partnership. Being business partners with your spouse will make the transition simpler because you know each other better. It will be able to communicate more honestly, leading to better decisions for the business' success. Additionally, you'll notice a significant improvement in your ability to communicate and listen professionally and personally.

- **Always there for one another**

Having a partner with whom to share your accomplishments and support one another through difficulties is the most valued advantage of starting a business together. You will be available for each other constantly to offer encouragement, come up with fresh ideas, and work on your projects all day long without becoming frustrated or bored.

- **Your marriage may take on a new level as a result.**

Being business partners as well as spouses, in the opinion of the majority, can give your marriage an entirely new dimension. In what way? Since you control the company, you have a greater stake in it than a hired employee. In addition, you are free to openly discuss delicate subjects with your spouse because you have complete trust in them, which makes this a perfect relationship. Also, you'll develop professionally with your spouse, which is a fantastic opportunity that brings irreplaceable joy.

- **You make your family's finances more stable.**

You can discuss your passion together with your spouse and produce something you can be proud of when you own a business together. If your company's goal is to secure your family's financial future, partnering with your marriage partner is the best for you because the full profit will go to the family. This is different when you have an outside party as your business partner, as you can never be on the same page together in your family's finances because they cannot understand your family's needs as your spouse will.

"Faith is that unknown, but we know it's there, faith is that first step into the darkness not knowing if it's going to be light on our journey. But I can assure you just as much as it will rain, so shall that sun rise; the first step is the hardest be strong King and Queens"

The challenges of working together with your marriage partner

Managing a business with your spouse undoubtedly has its difficulties. Every entrepreneur feels the strain of business growth. Some couples fear going into business with their partner because they discover that a business collaboration causes more conflict. However, this can be managed when the two parties are ready.

- **You find it hard to balance business and pleasure.**

When you co-own a company with your spouse, you can find it hard to separate your personal life from your work. While many people find that setting their schedule helps them achieve work-life balance, leaving work stuff at work can be difficult.

If you work and live together, it's possible that the stress of the job will affect your personal life and that you'll find yourself discussing work during family time. It might be challenging to draw distinctions between family and work-related difficulties. Additionally, it could lead to conflict and put your company under a lot of strain. With this guide's help, you'll learn how to balance your business and pleasure. Although it takes time as a process, constant consciousness of the practices will only produce the best result you have always desired.

Not knowing when to give each other space is another reason why a lot of people don't consider working alongside their spouses. Organizing the task can be difficult if you have skills and weaknesses in many areas.

"Whatever it is that you lost in wasn't really a lost, it was a learning opportunity so you can lose the appetite of losing and stop being a victim. It will be no "if only" when you're the one and only person responsible for your greatness"

Phases of partnering with your marriage partner

There are three phases you'll encounter when partnering with your spouse. Take note of each and compare them to know the current phase your home is now.

1. It first seems like it's going better than it's really going: At this stage, you really enjoy everything you do together with your spouse; It's like a honeymoon phase. Everything your partner does at home and at work seems to be very perfect for you, as you are still enjoying their companionship like it won't end.

2. Then there's a phase when it becomes hard for you to cope and spend the rest of your life with the same person; being your business partner and marriage partner. This is where a lot of work is required of you. I'll want you to understand first that it is normal for you to experience this; the person you can't stop singing their praise suddenly becomes tiring to you. Most people call it quit at this stage because they don't understand that all this stage requires is to press on and work on the big factors to help you see through this stage such as communication, role clarity, trust and not just backing out.

Business and Pleasure; eat your cake and have it

Having stayed clear on this second stage can help you achieve the maximum benefits of working with your marriage partner.

3. The stage where you unlock the full potential of working with your spouse: This is the most amazing phase when you've realized how much good you'll get with both business and pleasure. You spend so much of your time together in business and this also becomes your life as you are with your family.

CHAPTER THREE

LEADERSHIP AND FAMILY; SELF-REFLECTION

"Only if we knew that we were living in the good old days, would we truly appreciate what we have in the present"- Michael Carpenter.

You represent a larger part of your family you're your business. Leadership is an important role assumed by you and your spouse as the parents and the co-owner. Leadership entails guiding, working, managing, teaching the kids about values and beliefs, caring for, and supporting the family. It's a position of service for the family's growth and mutual development. The couple is tasked to create a formidable partnership and sense of importance for the kids to emulate and learn from.

Leaders should create a balance in meeting the needs of the family. There are situations where a total commitment is centered on a particular need, but we should learn when to be optimum with others in the relationship so as not to feel unwanted. Family bias should be well avoided so as not to hinder the normal growth process of others.

"We live for either ourselves or selfless for others."

When it comes to self-reflections the highest honor that can be esteemed upon a man of any social status or caliber is the title Father (Dad, Daddy, Papa). Truly makes you feel that you brought something into life that the world needs right now. When you feel unaccepted, your children will make you feel wanted, when you feel unaccomplished, look into your child eyes, and know that you have everything you need in this life.

There's a place where you must make certain changes that will keep your love alive and also produce the required result for your business. Let's quickly analyze what you can do to maintain balance and enjoy a successful family.

- **Create special time for special occasions:** Do you remember activities you engaged in before you could secure the hands of your spouse, all those gestures shown to each other to signify the level of love you have for one another before starting a family should be preserved like a culture. You can decide to reignite the old flames of love back then by revisiting some strategic locations in the past that molded you to bring about a family.

Ensure to find a perfect time that suits those occasions. You can even decide to take the whole family along and intrigue the kids about how you started with your spouse. Such stories always have a hilarious and enjoyable tone to them. Now, in practicality, you can choose the date that tallies with any of your birthdays, the day of your proposal, anniversaries, and special times should be fixed to go back the memory lane. Locations can be a restaurant, vacation, thanksgiving, where you met your spouse at first, where you both visit often, and anywhere that seems fun and triggers the good old days. Engaging in this occasionally is an excellent way to ensure balance in meeting different needs.

- **Engage in meditation:** meditation helps keep the body's state as calm as possible. Meditation also helps you see things from their point of view and question if your reaction was proper to such an event or attitude. Don't let your emotion get the best of you to keep malice, become violent, and distort every form of humanity in you. Let your brain and mind be the reactor instead of your body. Meditate enough to see the whole picture and how you can address it before going to bed that day. Meditation can come in the form of prayer, a quiet and alone time to think, a walk, or anything that gives you solace.

"Being thankful is more than just saying it, you must feel it, embrace it, nurture that feeling into everything in your life."

- **Please don't neglect the little things:** It's easier to trivialize things that we often encounter regularly or consider insignificant, especially when working with your spouse. We do not see the essence and importance when we don't put enough strength and understanding into it. We consider them normal and give ourselves a form of entitlement that shouldn't be at all.

Also, remember that these little things are what solidify a relationship. You can show in words and actions to appreciate your spouse. You don't have to organize a large party to show how much you care for your relationship; it can be as little as complimenting your partner concerning their jobs and commitment to the relationship.

Ask yourself these questions, when last did you celebrate your partner's or family's win? When last did you apologize and sincerely say sorry? Can you remember saying thank you for simply asking them to pass you your shoe? How well do you apologize? When was the last time you hugged your partner in public? When was the last time you planned a night out with your partner? How well do you communicate with your spouse? Do you offer a listening ear to your spouse? Many of these questions require your actions for the better. They sound easy and unimportant, but they ensure strong and cordial affection in a relationship. It's a suitable mode of balance to be practiced.

Business and Pleasure; eat your cake and have it

CHAPTER FOUR

TIME MANAGEMENT

"Not only is it possible for you to achieve your dreams but it is necessary"

The act of planning and constructing how to split and spend your time between various tasks set ahead of you is known as time management. If you are good at managing your time, you'll find that you work more efficiently and effectively to complete more tasks and satisfy both your home and business, even under time constraints and heavy pressure.

The technique of scheduling your free time and limiting the amount of time you devote to projects in order to perform more effectively is known as time management. Some people manage their time better than others, but everyone can acquire habits that will help them manage their time more effectively. Your work and home may suffer if you don't practice effective time management, which might result in the following:

- Putting out poor-quality work
- Increasing your level of stress
- Ruined business-pleasure life
- Damaging your reputation in the workplace
- Losing your marriage

"With every breath, one day it shall be a final exhale. Stay true to your potential and pay it forward to your dreams. I believe in you more then you believe in yourself. You owe it to yourself King and Queens to give every day 100 percent and work like tomorrow isn't promised Because It Isn't."

Sparing time for your partner and attending to your office tasks is much more difficult in our hectic lifestyle. Some couples struggle to efficiently manage their time, especially when working with their marriage partner. There is no justification for ignoring each other because of your hectic work schedules, regardless of whether you're just in a relationship or married.

The principles governing personal success are like professional success for partners working together, i.e., making a better partner at work and home can be easy even if you learn to be a better partner only at work or home. You need to set how to manage your time appropriately, spend it judiciously, and make sure your spouse is also doing the same thing so that it can be easier for you to make your marriage and your business work so that you can thrive and prosper together. As mentioned earlier, the challenges of co-running a business with your spouse increase when you don't know what to do and how to do it effectively.

"If you become frighten instead become inspired"

Time management strategies for couples working together

"You can't do what everyone else is doing and think you going to be great, you have to be transforming all the time"

- ➢ **Make a schedule of how each hour of your day will be spent**

Business and Pleasure; eat your cake and have it

To avoid running your day in confusion and lack of focus on what each minute and hour is meant to stand for, you need to schedule your day in advance. Setting up a timetable and keeping to it will enable you to attend to work as at when due and have fun with your spouse at the right time each day without feeling rushed or exhausted.

As you set to plan your time for each day, remember to write it down and let your partner be aware of how you've planned to spend the day. You'll be surprised at how unhurried your day may be if you take a few minutes the previous evening to set your schedule.

Ensure you also see them through the time management process by making them plan their day ahead. Even though you both lead busy lives, knowing what the other is doing at a specific time will help strengthen your bond, as it will be understandable before you explain how stressful it was after the day has ended. Get to stick with what your partner has in their calendar and allow them to schedule their time based on their assignment.

> **Don't work or flex nonstop all day.**

You need a balance between your work and your home. Even though you may be busy all day, try to make time to reach out to your partner every day for at least one hour. If you decide to spend the whole day on your work only, it will not be helpful to your home as this can make you and your partner drift apart in no time.

"In the face of the impossible become inspired"

The same thing applies to your business too, don't get distracted with your partner so much that you forget to carry out your set-down assignments. If a couple spends too much time together, it's too simple to lose respect. Spending too much time with your partner when you ought to be focused on work can make it challenging to control your emotions.

Please keep to how you've allocated each hour and try to carry them out without any faults. It may be challenging to stick to time management initially, but you'll get the best out of it if you practice and stay committed to it.

➢ **Make time for your sex life**.

Many couples find it challenging to continue their bedroom duties after the day has been spent with daily office duties. You must set aside time to engage physically and romantically with your partner and respect it. During that time, do whatever feels right. It might involve a massage, a shower, or in-depth sex.

This will help keep your marriage and help you maintain the energy in your home regardless of what happened at the office earlier that day.

> ➢ **Make time for yourself.**

Everyone requires some alone to get things straight with themselves. Even though spending time with your partner might be beneficial, having your office duties attended to is essential. Spend time alone, occasionally doing something you like to do yourself. You'll experience far greater calm and happiness.

Advantages of time management for couples working together

Time management is crucial in having a balanced business-pleasure life because it enables you to manage your workday and grow your business without jeopardizing your ability to maintain a healthy work-life balance. The following seven advantages of effective time management:

- **It helps you perform better.**

Having effective time management can help you have a better understanding of what you need to do at each given time, and you'll get to be aware of how long each task should take.

When you have a schedule to stick to, you'll definitely have what to do at hand, and you'll discover that you spend less time debating on specific tasks every time.

You will not be in a rush to do anything before a deadline that is rapidly approaching, and the quality of your work will improve.

"Adversity introduces you to the actual person you are"

- **Time management helps you improve your relationship**

Having an effective time management schedule can help you prioritize your home and work without having to deal with many flops. The most effective time management schedule is the one that helps you get a work-life balance, like ensuring that you have adequate time to finish each assignment and attend to your relationship timely.

- **Become less stressed**

Working without prioritizing what needs to be done will make you feel nervous about completing your tasks for both business and pleasure. Setting priorities for your projects and allowing yourself enough time to complete them will help you feel less stressed.

- **Increasing Your Confidence**

As an entrepreneur balancing work and pleasure, you'll get a sense of satisfaction and confidence in your skills when you successfully manage your time and meet your deadlines.

Finishing your daily to-do list consistently can also be a powerful motivation for you to advance your abilities.

"No sunrise without a sunset, there are no roses without rain"

Most important principles of time management

As mentioned earlier, developing your time management abilities can help you become more productive in all your assignments. You need to learn a few ways as an entrepreneur to help you grow your time management abilities.

- **Think ahead**

The key to effective time management is always to plan your time so that your tasks can be carried out perfectly. This can be best done by estimating how long it will take you to finish all the items on your to-do list for you to put them down and be conscious of the next day from the day you plan. Planning is one thing and being conscious of your tasks is another. Ensure you are ready to stay faithful to yourself and stay in line with getting the best result from your time management abilities.

- **Set tasks' priorities**

Determine which tasks are the most urgent and important for each project you need to focus on, then give those your top priority for the day. If you are the most productive at midnight, plan your most crucial roles until midnight so that you can maximize the period to work effectively. Schedule your simple and fewer chores when you are less active. This can be best done by studying yourself and knowing what works well for you.

"I am no longer blocking anymore of my blessings. I will no longer say I didn't do anything different; I will no longer say I'm just like such and such because I am not the same. I am different. I move different I hustle I cry but I stand tall in every room I enter, and I am Triumphant because I never give up. Failure is not an option because, I made a commitment to my family that until my last breath every dream will come true, every Barrier will be crossed, and every obstacle will be overcame. I am very humble, and you will never know my social status unless I tell you, but don't get it twisted I am the best at what I do and it's okay to say your blessed. You are different and you are not like anyone else because you're not. You are you and it's okay to be blessed."

Business and Pleasure; eat your cake and have it

Mr. Gentleman

CHAPTER FIVE

THE SMART MOVE

"Stop pressing replay on the things that need to be deleted from your life"

Setting boundaries

Creating healthy boundaries is essential for your relationship and work because they help you to preserve a balance between you and your partner. Setting healthy boundaries helps to reduce your conflicts and arguments because they set expectations for what you can anticipate from one another. This can also strengthen your relationship with your partner at home and work. Boundaries are essential for every couple partnering as entrepreneurs because they provide both the room to complete their tasks independently.

When a couple must live together for an extended period, time and space are crucial to their mental health. Setting healthy boundaries in your work-love life doesn't mean you will shut off communication or ignore your partner for some time and then return to normal after a given period. No!

Creating healthy boundaries means giving each other some healthy time to engage in your personal way or otherwise spend your time as you may wish. Boundaries don't call for ignoring, it only calls for some respect to be put in place, and this can be best done by taking it in the slightest way possible. By doing things their way, your partner will feel more valuable in their own eyes, boosting their comfort and ease with themselves. So, to maintain your relationship and work, here are some strategies to define these healthy boundaries.

1. Consider designating specific times during the workday for no interactions.

Giving yourself sometime during the workday for no interaction is very important for setting healthy boundaries between you and your business partner, who's also your marriage partner. This can be done at any time when you know you need to be alone to reason about some important tasks ahead of you or to handle your assigned or set-down task, such as during lunch and any short breaks. These restrictions can assist you in concentrating on your work and continuing to be effective in the duties you oversee. Additionally, you can gain something from the time apart, making you value your time spent together after work even more.

2. Make distinct and unique workspaces according to your best office setup.

To simulate the atmosphere of an office, consider setting up two separate workspaces if you can: one for you and the other for your partner. This will help you stay more focused, motivated, productive, and creative.

Even if you both work for the same firm and work together from home, you need to create a separate workspace based on how you'll love your space to be and how it will be convenient for you to handle your assignments effectively. Ensure your spouse also pick their unique settings and decoration for the workspace and try not to influence their decision.

Working together in this fashion can be advantageous for several reasons, including the opportunity to maintain a consistent schedule. When you and your partner are working from the comfort of your home, it may be alluring to talk to one another, but keeping the separation that an office setting would provide can also be advantageous to your relationship because it promotes a healthy business-pleasure balance.

> *"It's always going to be a rainy day no matter who you are, but you can either dance in the rain or just get wet"*

3. Form a plan to manage your stress

When your life partner is also your business partner, it is even more crucial that you can handle the stress that comes with beginning your own company.

> *"When you are faithful over someone else, God will give you your own"*

Just as it is unavoidable in relationships, stress is an element of beginning and operating a business. It can be even harder if you're not used to working with your partner on a professional level. Therefore you and your spouse should create a stress management strategy that includes techniques that promote relaxation (such as deep abdominal breathing, visualization, and yoga), strategies for framing and talking about irrational thoughts (such as a thorough communication plan), and a set timeout period where, if a situation becomes too intense, you both go for a 15-minute walk separately before returning to resume communication.

4. Schedule Business Meetings with Your Partner.

"It's necessary to associate yourself with winners."

A simple mistake most couple entrepreneurs make is that having a business meeting with your business partner isn't necessary because you have full access to each other. Setting up business meetings where you have the floor to discuss important concerns of your business might be helpful for you as an entrepreneur partnering with your spouse. Like you'll schedule business meetings with your coworkers, ensure you do the same with your partner. Let there be an agenda for the meeting, progress report, and deliverables.

This extends past the hasty, tactical sessions to address a particular issue. Decide on a specific time in your calendars and remember to be just as prepared as you would be for another one-on-one business meeting with another colleague.

Hold a quick recap meeting in the evening before the end of the working day, if necessary, to address any problems that have arisen. Hold these meetings in your office if possible. This way, if there is a conflict, you can both literally and figuratively leave the point of contention behind when you return to your common space as a couple after going home for the evening.

5. Prioritize your emotional wellbeing

By prioritizing your emotional well-being, you may avoid losing your identity or sense of self. Because your position as a healthy individual greatly influences the entire health of your relationship, you must protect and nurture your mental health.

You maintain a strong connection with your mate by taking care of your heart and soul. You may keep a close relationship with your partner by caring for your heart and soul. The easiest way to keep a healthy relationship is to

Business and Pleasure; eat your cake and have it

achieve your goals and desires because you'll learn to love yourself more and see your partner as an equal.

CHAPTER SIX

STORIES FROM SUCCESSFUL BUSINESSES MANAGED BY COUPLES (CASE STUDY; Cathy and Jeffrey, Vernic and Mitesh, David and Nicole)

"You keep saying to yourself that you not on the next level because X, Y, Z.. The truth of the matter is, you aren't there because you aren't there".

➤ Cathy and Jeffrey, The owners of Hillock Estate Distillery

They work at their business, Hillock Estate Distillery, which is a chill 100 miles outside of New York City on a farm in the Hudson Valley. This lovely entrepreneur and couple met 22 years ago, and they bought their farm in 1999. They started the land with rice, barley, and corn. Making them a producer of whiskey since 2011.

They've discovered that they have both been incredible and diligent workers for them to be able to achieve this success. They have three sons, and their family is passionate and committed to what they do. They understand each other's schedules and personalities at work and home, which has helped them have time to spend together as a family.

They have learned about the importance of effective communication so far, and the chance they had to collaborate and launch a firm has taught them how crucial effective communication and delegation are to their professional success. Sales, marketing, distribution, and events fall within Catty's purview while Jeffrey oversees farming, operations, finances, and whiskey manufacturing.

Vernic & Mitesh, Founders of PlantOGram

Vernic and Mitesh run a gifting business with headquarters in Hollywood that sends out fully grown trees and plants, PlantOGram. This company produces non-GMO fruits every year, which can be cultivated in your house or apartment.

Their path crossed first in the early 2000s, and they finally took it to another level and got wedded officially in 2005. They didn't just stop as marriage partners but also made the decision to make their green thumb for fruit trees their full-time business in 2007

By starting a business, Mitesh and his wife have discovered far more about themselves as a relationship than they had anticipated. He has once in his speech expatiate that each of them is powerful on their own and, when combined, will produce a force of kindness attacking you. "We can truly appreciate one another for the unique aspirations we each have and for how we may bring these goals together to create a better, more sustainable life,"

Business and Pleasure; eat your cake and have it

Much like being in a relationship, Mitesh said the most important lesson was discovering methods to utilize each other's strengths.

By the virtue of delegating roles, they've combined their abilities to create one of the most recognizable businesses in the charitable sector today.

Their first piece of advice is to be patient. "Don't worry about the little things. They are only stuff, after all, and what matters is how strongly you are committed to one another and how that will distinguish your company as one of the greatest in its field. Above all, remember to make time for one another. Dinner, movie nights, or simply a simple mall stroll. This is not the time to conduct business; instead, Mitesh advises that you connect and take stock of your relationship and the distance you have traveled together.

"Consider yourself the apex of your craft"

David and Nicole, The Cookie Cups

Their business, The Cookie Cups, is situated in Minneapolis, Minnesota. These popular sweet snacks are easy to consume and resemble cookies in part but are actually cupcake shaped. They met in 2012 in Las Vegas and initially launched an online jewelry store in 2014, then changed course to launch The Cookie Cups in 2015.

Having a one-year-old daughter and an almost four-year-old business, they have discovered the value of choosing your battles in their relationship. "We won't always agree, and things won't always turn out as we hoped. Sometimes I try to ignore the conflict, concentrate on something more important, and move on by biting my tongue. Although David and I enjoy having lighthearted disagreements, he is incredibly devoted to and loves our family without condition, says Nicole.

They advised you always to remember that disagreement is acceptable and beneficial, as it opens room to see from another perspective. "Starting a business with a partner can be highly beneficial but also very difficult at times. You

Business and Pleasure; eat your cake and have it

must learn to disagree and keep your relationships intact even if you don't always agree. You also can't work nonstop.

CHAPTER SEVEN

THE BUSINESS AND PLEASURE BALANCE RESPONSIBILITIES

"Marriage (relationships) is a marathon, not a race. If you want to survive the test of time you have to work for it. It makes it so much sweeter."

Show more extraordinary passion and enthusiasm toward your relationship.

As an entrepreneur finding a balance between business and pleasure, you must grow and show a long passion for your relationship. Showing passion towards your relationship is mainly when you experience sexual desire and powerful emotion towards your partner. This type of love is often associated with the start of a relationship, so many couples lack passion as they proceed in their love journey.

The bond you have with your partner is the most significant one in your life. If you can remember the early stage and how you started, those periods you spent hours conversing with them because you are curious about everything. You frequently fantasize about their day and night and wish you could be with them all the time; that's the passion.

Couples that work together need to be passionate about their relationship and making it work because passion fades, and mostly it fades with time. Keep in mind that once your passion for your partner fades, it can no longer be feigned, and this can lead to a loss of attention at work because you won't want to spend any time with your spouse.

Passion can be rekindled by making some moves that can keep the flame of love burning in your union. The truth about keeping a marriage remains that your partner loves to see you passionate about them and the things you have in common. And it's essential when you and your partner are beginning or expanding a business.

"Complacency engulfs us all when we are comfortable but shame on the Leader for getting complacent because of their title"

To grow your passion,

- Keep in mind what you did to build your relationship, and it will require you to continue.
- Keep using the same lovely names you started with to address your partner.
- At the beginning of your relationship, if you compliment them on even the most minor thing, ensure you continue doing so.
- Do a minimum of one date every month without discussing work.
- Put your phones on silent, unplug, and spend time together.

"You want to max out your humanity by using your energy to lift yourself up to your family and the people around you"

Signs of a passionate couple working together

1. You adore every aspect of one another.

This simply means that you are aware of your partner's flaws and shortcomings, yet you still adore them. You can show your partner you are passionate about your relationship by making them feel significant.

2. You anticipate a bright future together.

As a passionate couple, having a shared vision can be very effective. A crucial indicator of passion in a relationship is when you share a common vision and are ready to support each other.

3. You give up things for one another.

Giving is the key to a passionate relationship because it satisfies the sixth human need. The secret of being passionate about your partner is the life you get when you give up things for them. By doing so, you give them life and make them see reasons to proceed further in their confidence.

4. You two are friendly to one another.

Touch is intimate; even seemingly insignificant acts, such as holding hands while walking or patting your spouse on the knee while you sit next to one other, show how deeply you are bonded.

5. You are free to express yourself. It can also mean expressing unfavorable emotions without worrying that your partner will behave impulsively. You are able to converse effectively and settle disputes peacefully, allowing you to express your emotions without fear.

6. Your partner inspires you. They encourage you to develop and advance as a person. The sixth need of humans is growth. If you're not developing, you're dying, which also goes for your relationship.

7. You're determined to make it happen. Relationships can sometimes lose their passion because of life events. But one of the characteristics of a passionate relationship is that you will notice it, talk about it, and fix it.

Be eager to apologize.

"Quiet using the word luck and start using the word work. Start believing in the results of your actions"

Saying sorry can be challenging, especially when you can't find enough reason as a backup for your apology. When you apologize to your partner, you could feel inadequate because an apology makes an individual feel as if they are admitting that they are flawed rather than just having done something wrong.

However, a well-delivered, adequately honest apology will typically avoid all these problems and help instead to bring in a resolution, reinforce shared values, and restore positive feelings. All you need to know is when and how to apologize.

"I have enough. I've done enough. I am enough,"

Essential to apologize sincerely to your partner

- Take Charge of Your Behavior

You don't have to accept blame for mistakes that weren't your fault if you apologize. You can apologize for accidentally upsetting someone's feelings. Still, you don't have to add words that can make the person feel less of themselves, like 'I didn't expect that you'll do this, with your level of knowledge" if you genuinely believe you had no means of foreseeing that your actions would do them harm.

While accepting responsibility may also require subtly bringing up actions that you believe were right on your part, it is also necessary for you to attempt to identify what you did that you believe is wrong. By doing this, you shield yourself from the perception that if you are the first to apologize, you accept blame for the entire issue or most of it because it is not so.

- Say, "I'm sorry."

Don't try to justify your actions or qualify your apologies. Don't waste your important time carrying on a debate on why you should apologize. Many people are with an apologizing mindset, but they spend most of the time justifying their actions. To balance your business-pleasure life, just say "I'm sorry" in its place.

A sincere apology can be described as simple and straightforward, but it is advised that you study your partner at home and work to know the best way to apologize. Apologizing is not necessarily admitting that you made a mistake to apologize. It could be a conscious action to admit that you wronged someone else.

"Everything about you is great stop choosing to be average"

Learn to forgive

"You can hear the siren call you to the rocks without crashing into the rocks"

In a relationship where you work with your partner, forgiveness is needed to live a separation-free and balanced life. Forgiveness, in this sense, means altering your feelings, plans, desires, and ideas toward your spouse. It entails embracing positive feelings and vibes only (for example, empathy and goodwill) and letting go of bad and negative vibes (e.g., grudges, less desire for retribution and retaliation, wrath, conflict, and bitterness) toward your partner.

Forgiveness isn't compulsorily accepting or approving the offense. It is only a way to let your partner know they deserve you. You can feel happier in your relationship, keep it going through difficult times, achieve your marital goals, and improve its performance with forgiveness. Your physical, natural, emotional, and psychological health can all benefit greatly by forgiving your partner. Additionally, even though it could be simpler to forgive when the offender apologizes, you don't always need to wait. Remember that you both are required to put in effort for this to work out, so you can still forgive if your spouse doesn't.

But remember that it takes time to forgive. It can sometimes be hard. You might have often wanted it to be a quick choice for your issue, but you'll discover that it is more complicated than what you can do effortlessly. Forgiveness is a gradual process, and every couple working together needs it to strike a balance between the double life. Keep in mind that if you decide to forgive your partner, it will be of more benefit to you and what you've shared.

Be open to communication.

"Royalty is in the sky, and we must have that burning desire to jump and reach it"

For you to have a balanced business-pleasure life, communication is necessary. While it's OK to inquire about your partner's day, you need to go deeper than small conversations if you want an outstanding connection with them. Effective communication for spouses working together involves learning to listen rather than talk in your relationship. Many people don't understand why communication is important, so they ignore the chances of making things right.

Why is communication important in relationships?

Since you spend most of your time with your partner in the office, there is a higher chance of misunderstandings and arguments. But you can make the best out of this when you understand and master communication.

➢ IMPROVED TRUST

For couples working together, true communication is essential because you can talk to your spouse about anything, including your joys and sorrows, good days and bad. Since you are confident in their unwavering love and support, you will be trusted more.

➢ BETTER DISPUTE RESOLUTION

Even though every relationship has its ups and downs, frequent fighting, and the absence of any fighting at all are indicators of poor communication in relationships. Effective communication helps settle disputes easily. This means that when conflicts arise, you'll be able to use them to build up rather than destroy your relationship.

➢ GROWING INTIMACY

Practicing effective communication will greatly improve your ability to listen, comprehend, and sympathize with your spouse. This demonstrates your regard for and appreciation for your partner's thoughts and opinions. There's a level of emotional intimacy that frequently follows physical closeness with your spouse.

"Money is little more than a cartoon in the brain that we're addicted to watching".

Communication skills for relationships

How to improve your communication skills to strike a balance between your work and home life After learning how important it is to communicate well at home, you should make an extra effort to improve yourself and find a balance between work and pleasure.

1. **Engage in true connection**
The idea that communicating in a relationship is the same as talking or having a discussion is the biggest myth. Relationship communication is fundamentally about connecting with your spouse and using your verbal, written, and physical abilities to meet their needs. There is no need to engage in small talk. It's important to see things from your

partner's point of view, give them support, and let them know you're their biggest fan.

> *"Remember to enjoy your life, your family and those you call friends. You owe it to not just yourself but humanity. Experience everyday like it must be lived, or your time will not count".*

Particularly in long-term partnerships, it is easy to allow genuine connection and desire to wane. But once you can sense that you aren't communicating as well as you should, admitting that you're not connecting as much as you used to is the first step in learning how to enhance communication in a relationship. You need to admit and be conscious of the fact that you must work on that. Discuss how to rekindle your relationship with your partner and offer a starting point. Don't worry if your partner isn't on board. Relationships are places you go to offer rather than take, so you are doing the right thing if you sacrifice for your relationship.

Relationships and communication are both distinct. Recognizing this will help you and your partner communicate effectively. You must pay attention to how your partner communicates with you; With this, you have the chance to avoid frustration and develop intimacy and trust.

Watch your partner's reactions to various perceptual cues for a day or two while you work to improve your communication skills. Do they appear to react best when they are looking and seeing? Speaking? or by doing and touching? Making a lot of eye contact and using subtle facial expressions, for instance, may be less effective in establishing a connection with your partner if they respond more to language, tone, and other aural cues. Although you are sending signals, they are not receiving them. On the other hand, keep in mind that simply saying "I love you" might not be sufficient if you discover that you are an auditory person, and your partner is a kinesthetic person. Remind yourself to touch frequently to express your love.

Business and Pleasure; eat your cake and have it

Role clarity

"If you find what's wrong with everything you have you can never have favor, if you find what's right with everything you have you can unlock the full potential of universe"

Entrepreneurs are used to wearing many hats and doing many different things, especially at the start of a business. Make sure you are not carrying out the same tasks as your partner if you desire to operate together. These distinct divisions are necessary for you to be more productive and will likely lead to clarity at best or intense conflict at worst.

Of course, dividing out the many tasks in a young company can be difficult in and of itself. A good place to start is by considering your background, prior experience, natural talents, and the things that thrill you the most. If you perform duties that are a good fit for you, you will each have a lot higher chance of maintaining the intensity of start-up life.

Who does what depends entirely on you, your partner, and the needs of your business, but minimizing the overlap between your areas of responsibility will help you work together more effectively and avoid conflict.

Having such a clear idea of what you need to do will help you a lot with the second important issue, which is empowerment at work.

Having faith in, respecting, and empowering your spouse Couples that argue over business matters frequently do so because one partner struggles to trust the other to carry out their obligations fully. One partner often criticizes the other's judgments, badgers him to complete a task, or takes on duties that belong to the other.

Unsurprisingly, these conflicts at work frequently spill over into the family. If something goes wrong at work and you blame your spouse for it, you won't want to be all cuddly with the same person you're upset with, as one lady who co-owned a real estate company with her husband told me.

Make sure to provide honest responses to the following questions if you and your spouse want to work together on the venture: Do I believe my partner is doing his job? Can I allow her to decide for herself? Can I allow him to do his work in the manner and in the time frame that he believes to be ideal? Can I let go enough to let my wife take full responsibility for her role?

> *"Don't forget, though, that you come from a long, unbroken line of ancestors who survived unimaginable adversity, difficulty, and struggle. It's their genes and their blood that run through your body right now. Without them, you wouldn't be here."*

Letting your significant other have complete power is more challenging than it sounds. Most business owners find it difficult to give up some control, which is what this necessitates. If you are unable to relinquish control, your partner may view your interference as contempt, which could ruin any commercial relations.

> *"Most rather live with regrets, and if your most people then live in the minority"*

If you can't let go of control, your partner will see your intrusion as a sign of disrespect.

The truth is that working alongside your partner will always come with hazards. More often than partners who don't cooperate, you will likely disagree, fight, and injure one another. However, if you handle this disagreement correctly by paying attention, showing respect, and showing empathy, there's a good possibility the tension will eventually make your relationship stronger.

Everyone's not doing everything. Just do well to organize everything so your partner is aware of their functions and office and same as you. There should be things that you autonomously do and things that your partner autonomously do too. Keep in mind that it is needed of you to have real clarity on roles. Because if this isn't done, you are going to feel like you either have no power or all the power and this will make your business partner really upset.

After that, both your marriage and your business will prosper.

Business and Pleasure; eat your cake and have it

"Count your blessing while you're in the blessing while you're experiencing the blessing not when it's too late or you hit rock bottom."

Love and Finances

Marriage is a business relationship, and finances are a big part involved in growing that partnership. Remember that the course is about business and pleasure; both require a critical assessment of funding(financing) to build and promote them.

Research conducted by fidelity investments stated that about 61% of couples discuss their finances monthly, which has gradually decreased over the years. Finances are a major and important discussion for couples to balance their assets and liabilities. Any partnership business, including that between a couple, requires finances to promote the relationship. It's evident that specific needs require proper finances, like getting a house, owning a car, planning vacations, and starting a family are why finances are essential in a marriage.

A survey by AICPA also proved that Financial' infidelity' is enough to end 2 in 5 relationships. Also, a major leading disagreement between couples is related to finances, as about 70% of relationships undergo this issue. Remember that one of the altars promises you agreed to was for richer or poorer, but you can plan the extent of each extremity by planning.

So, what can you do with your finances if you are about to get married or have already married?

- **Be plain about your finances:** Communication matters for couples because it's the only way to understand each other better. Select a time to talk about your finances during one of the numerous dates you have. Start with your financial status (if you owe a debt and what your monthly income is), discuss your financial goals and how you plan to achieve them, and talk about your spending habits so you can see if it works for you as well or you can arrive at a consensus on the limit you are to engage in either weekly, monthly, or yearly. There will be compromises that you will require to attain that level of spending. Engage in discussions about how your family spends and the budgets in which you were raised. This is to ensure the dependent attitudes of each other and to have an idea of what you are getting into. The truth is that this stage brings about conflict when you both start because there might be some differences, but with time, you both remind yourself why you decided to stick to these habits and goals, which will drive you to speak about it more.

"If you think it-you won't, if you believe it- you might, if you live it-you will"

- **Understand your assets and liabilities:** Ensure that you take note of your weekly or monthly assets and liabilities as partners. This is majorly for married folks. Discuss your financial streams of income and expenditure. See how well you've invested in assets and if your liabilities are becoming too much to check each other on how to curb the liabilities. In fact, ensure to know your net worth by removing your debts from your total asset in cash, stocks, investments, and other income streams. Once you check through your savings, then move on to the next step below.

- **Create a joint account:** You both are accustomed to how you deal with your finances. The following action Is how to combine finances as partners. The best way to start a joint account is an account that can be subjected to changes. To open such an account, first, deduct the liabilities and expenses you might need from your income before depositing them in the joint account. Ensure you deduct the tax, utilities, debts, health insurance, grocery goods, and other expenses from your mainstream income and deposit the rest in the joint account.

I'm sure you noticed that miscellaneous funds like unexpected expenses that could show up should also be added to the expenses before depositing the remaining funds in the joint account. Now, the changes that You can subject the joint account to may require a budgeted amount that you can decide to use for your wants and get whatever you desire.

- **Set financial goals:** You will do the following activities with the joint account. This is when you plan on short-term or long-term goals on what to achieve with the account. Do you want to buy a yacht, a vacation out of the country, a new car, invest with more enormous funds and safer stock or hedge funds, or pay for a good ivy league for your kids? Whatever it is, always reduce your liabilities to as much as possible to actualize your goals faster. Be smart with funds to ascertain a good credit score. Although a good credit score predisposes you to borrow money better, the goal here is to reduce debts and liabilities.

A problem often encountered with joint accounts is the disparity in goals. Goals are often different between spouses, and student loans place a considerable toil on the joint account that should be worked on. It's best if they stick to a decision on how each could split the money from the joint savings account and achieve whatever it is separately. But the rule remains that withdrawal should be simultaneous for you both.

CONCLUSION

Partnering with your spouse to set up a business can be easy if you get the right step to manage your business and pleasure life. Keep in mind that you both need to work towards perfection.

I understand that this point you are is seeming difficult to move and detrimental to your business but be calm this shall pass. It is a path you must pass; very important. There is a reason you and your partner have this unspoken void right now. It's because you are focusing on leveling up as individuals but not together. You can't reach greatness without breathing, praying (meditation) as one unit. Enjoy those unspoken nights on the couch, eventually that partner will look like a close friend you live with.

It is achievable if you are intentional about it. Good luck to you and your partner!

www.ingramcontent.com/pod-product-compliance
Lightning Source LLC
Chambersburg PA
CBHW020455220526
45464CB00002B/994